Titanic: Touchstones of a Tragedy

Titanic: Touchstones of a Tragedy

The timeless human drama revisited through period artifacts and memorabilia

Steve A Santini

Writers Club Press
San Jose New York Lincoln Shanghai

Titanic: Touchstones of a Tragedy
The timeless human drama revisited through period artifacts
and memorabilia

Writers Club Press
an imprint of iUniverse.com, Inc.

For information address:
iUniverse.com, Inc.
620 North 48th Street, Suite 201
Lincoln, NE 68504-3467
www.iuniverse.com

ISBN: 0-595-12649-9

Printed in the United States of America

For Craig, Gary, and Tony—

Titanic collectors, maritime researchers, and more importantly, my friends,

and

My Uncle Steve—

who, through a simple yet moving gift, opened a young man's eyes

to the wondrous power of words.

Contents

List of Illustrations

Every effort has been made to correctly attribute all material reproduced in this book. All items and images pictured in this volume are the property of the Titanic Concepts Inc.

Front and rear cover designs: Jason Halstead

Chapter One

1. Period White Star advertisement, photographed by Fran Sanagan

2. Nineteenth century passenger list, photographed by F. Sanagan

3. Canvas ticket wallet, photographed by F. Sanagan

4. *Adriatic* passenger list from first decade of twentieth century, photographed by F. Sanagan

5. White Star Line officer's cap, photographed by F. Sanagan

6. *Cretic* menu, 1913, photographed by F. Sanagan

Chapter Two

1. Period photograph of the Great Gantry, Belfast, photographed by F. Sanagan

2. English white oak newel post face from *Olympic's* great staircase, photographed by F. Sanagan

3. White Star Line promotional booklet for *Olympic*, photographed by F. Sanagan

4. *Olympic* postcard, photographed by F. Sanagan

5. Crystal menu holder with White Star burgee motif, photographed by F. Sanagan

6. *Olympic* third class ticket, c.1920, photographed by F. Sanagan

Chapter Three

1. Photo card of the Great Gantry, Belfast, photographed by F. Sanagan

2. Envelope from White Star Line head office, Liverpool, c.1910, photographed by F. Sanagan

3. White Star Line promotional pamplet, 1912, photographed by F. Sanagan

4. Cadbury chocolate card, photographed by F. Sanagan

Foreword

On April 15, 1999, eighty-seven years after the most luxurious ship in the world was last seen afloat in the North Atlantic Ocean, the Manitoba Museum of the Titanic opened its doors. In these pages, *Titanic*'s history is compellingly illustrated through the items of the museum's extraordinary and previously unpublished collection of rare letters, photographs, documents, china, woodwork, and more. Via these cogent reminders of the past, this book touches upon such timeless issues as heroism and cowardice and the conflict between the forces of nature and the power of technology.

Titanic: Touchstones of a Tragedy is, in essence, a handy museum of the doomed behemoth between two book covers. And Author Steve Santini, who has impeccably researched each artifact, is the virtual tour guide through the following pages. Santini's perspective is refreshingly unique as he presents a poignant and easy-to-understand account of the *Titanic*'s saga from the story of the company which built her to the ship's final hours and beyond into history and myth. By means of the museum's artifacts utilized in the book, the reader is vicariously transported back aboard the ship. For instance, one might catch a glimpse of first class passengers descending the aft grand staircase, steadying themselves along its elegant wooden handrail, a portion of which is featured in this book. Others may find themselves quietly observing a passenger whiling away the hours with a good book on the very deck chair seen in these pages, about which Santini writes with the wisdom and passion of a fine craftsman. The opportunity to marvel at the opulence of the great ship thanks to the items presented within Santini's book is like a dream come true.

The end of the *Titanic* signaled both the demise of the gilded age, in which wealth and privilege reigned supreme, and the beginning of an era marked by an intense curiosity about every aspect of the doomed luxury liner. *Titanic: Touchstones of a Tragedy* brings us as close as we have come to quenching that thirst for knowledge.

Craig A. Sopin, Philadelphia, 2000

Acknowledgments

The idea for a book in which actual *Titanic*-related artifacts would illustrate the tragic tale of the doomed ship has been with me for many years. Countless were the times I would sit down to begin work on this project only to be distracted, called to another matter, or have my faith in the 'Titanic community' shaken and tested by critics and detractors.

Ironically, it has been some of these very same critics and detractors who have provided me the most support. Time and again they have shown me that just because one holds the title of curator, scientist, historian, or expert, it does not necessarily mean any one person is capable of knowing everything about the *Titanic*, or articles related to the ill-fated ocean liner. To put it simply, none of us were there that cold April night, but all of us are capable of making errors in judgment regardless of the degree we may possess. Like the *Titanic's* passengers, we too are only human.

There are, however, some individuals of influence who have offered support to all of my *Titanic*-related endeavors. Of note are Canadian scientist and environmentalist Dr. Joseph B. MacInnis, and curator/director of the Bruce County Museum and Archives, Mrs. Barbara Ribey. To both exceptional people, I send my sincerest thanks. Others who have assisted and encouraged me over the years and are deserving of thanks include, David Archibald, Norm Ribey and the entire Ribey clan, 'Big John' and Karen, Bill Ricks, Dave and Betty King, Ken Marschall and Vern Shrock, Greg Cochkanoff, Tony Probst, Craig and Ruth Sopin, Gary Robinson, Rich Romano, Ered Matthews of

Cabin Class Collectibles, Dave and Sam Peter, Al and Susan Collins, and—of course—Mom, Dad, and Leslie.

Assisting with the actual book and most in line for thanks are; my editor, Jason Halstead, who not only proof read the manuscript, but also prepared the layout, images, and cover design, and photographers Craig Ward, Fred Greenslade, and Fran Sanagan.

Last, but certainly not least (I believe in saving the best for last), I send my heartfelt love and respect to Ms. Vera Hermanns, owner of the Titanic Concepts Inc. collection and, more importantly, my partner in life. Words cannot describe the good fortune bestowed on an individual who is able to find not only a soul mate, but another person who believes in their own dream and is willing to climb aboard to share the experience. Whether seas have been calm or rough, Vera has always been there to make sure I stay 'on course and full steam ahead,' at times when I would have gladly headed straight for the lifeboats to abandon ship. Thank you Vera, for being with me, and more importantly, for being the special person you are.

Steve Santini

Introduction

She has endured the passage of time and has cast her spell over millions of people worldwide. She is the legendary *RMS Titanic*. From her icy grave more than two miles beneath the Atlantic Ocean this grand old lady continues to fascinate and intrigue. Explorers have spent million of dollars to find her, salvage crews have dreamed of her treasures, and Hollywood has immortalized her in countless films and documentaries. Why is this? What is it about this single shipwreck that so compels us?

Perhaps the answer lies rooted in the fact that the *Titanic* disaster was, and is, a very *human* story. As the sloping decks of the massive liner gradually surrendered to the icy embrace of the sea, people were faced with choices. Choices of how to behave, how to survive, and in many cases, how to perish. Incredibly, even though three-quarters of a century have elapsed since that tragic April night, it would appear that many of us can somehow identify with those choices.

For others, not captivated or moved by the *Titanic's* tale, it is difficult to experience with any degree of empathy the true effect of this monumental disaster. Given that our television screens are filled on a nightly basis with images of death and destruction, the loss of human life on the *Titanic* seems for many a dim and distant event, unworthy of sympathy or even a passing understanding. After all, many of us know we will never face such a catastrophe. Many of us were not alive when the *Titanic* went to the bottom, most of us do not know a single soul from the doomed ship. This detachment makes it almost effortlessly possible to replace the emotion and fear of real people with the fictitious antics of Hollywood actors paid to present this piece of history to the masses on the silver screen.

This book is an attempt to reattach hearts and imaginations to the true events surrounding the loss of the *Titanic*. Through numerous images of rare objects related to the *Titanic*, this work sets out to retell a very familiar tale in a unique and personal way that puts a human face on the disaster. In this context, these ordinary items connected with an extraordinary historical event take on a new life. They speak to us in a quiet yet profound way which the passage of time has done little to diminish.

In writing this book, I have decided to allow the artifacts to play the major role in the telling of the *Titanic's* tale. These fragile yet tangible slivers of time continue to remind us that what took place on April 15, 1912 was a truly *human* experience.

I

Shining Star
The Titanic's owners, the White Star Line

The late nineteenth century and early twentieth century were heady times for transatlantic steamship companies. With the immigrant tide to the New World reaching its zenith in this era, the principal players in the ocean transport trade each sought to outdo the other with the creation of bigger and faster vessels in which they could carry passengers across the North Atlantic Ocean. In many ways, this need for evolution in the size and the appointments of the ships in the various fleets was a welcome development, especially for anyone actually planning an ocean crossing.

Prior to the many creature comforts this new competitive spirit produced, ocean travel was often a hazardous and less than sanitary undertaking. On board the early ocean steamships, there was often only one traveling class known as 'saloon class.' All passengers, regardless of wealth or social standing, shared common public areas on board, areas where communicable diseases came to flourish and be easily passed on. The mortality rate on early steamships, especially among infants, was high. Live cattle were carried on board to provide fresh meat and milk and the sleeping quarters were, as one critic of the time observed, "little more spacious than coffins."

Adding to the peril of early crossings was the lack of functional radio equipment with which to signal for assistance should a ship meet with trouble. Indeed, quite often vessels left port simply never to be heard from again, leaving no clue as to the fate that had befallen them. Fortunately, the passage of time and improvements in the state of the art saw many revisions introduced to make a passenger's voyage both safer and more comfortable.

The year 1900 dawned upon fierce competition between a number of steamship companies all striving for the lion's share of the lucrative North Atlantic passenger trade. One of the leading firms doing battle in this highly changed commercial arena was the White Star Line (Oceanic Steam Navigation Company).

Founded in 1869 by Thomas Henry Ismay, the White Star Line was a British firm operating in direct competition with its principal rival, the Cunard Steamship Company Ltd., and also facing off with a number of leading German and continental steamship lines. Originally, Ismay had planned to offer near exclusive steamship service to Australia but the Belfast ship building firm of Harland and Wolff convinced the White Star founder that the vessels they could construct for his line would be better suited to the highly profitable North Atlantic run between Europe and North America.

Thus began a long and profitable working relationship between Harland and Wolff and the White Star Line with the Belfast company building nearly all of the ships in Ismay's fleet. In the opinion of many historians, the vessels constructed by Harland and Wolff were among the most graceful and sleek of any transatlantic liners before or since. On most of the ships, the profile of the vessel showed a trim, yacht-like line that completely offset the massive size of the ships.

It was not only in hull design that the Harland and Wolff ships were elegant. Through a slow but steady evolution, White Star became known for the comfort and luxury of its ships. Gone were the dingy common rooms of the early steamers, replaced by first class staterooms and public areas boasting cut crystal light fixtures and magnificent carved wooden accents. Also improved were the dining facilities and the quality of meals served on board. In time, the service and cuisine of White Star ships rivaled that of the finest hotels and restaurants in both Europe and America and the line emerged to become a firm favorite with transatlantic travelers.

All of this progress was threatened with collapse when, in 1906, White Star was presented with a serious threat in the form of two new ships—the *Lusitania* and the *Mauritania*—conceived by Ismay's old rival, Cunard. The 'space race' of oceanic transport was underway.

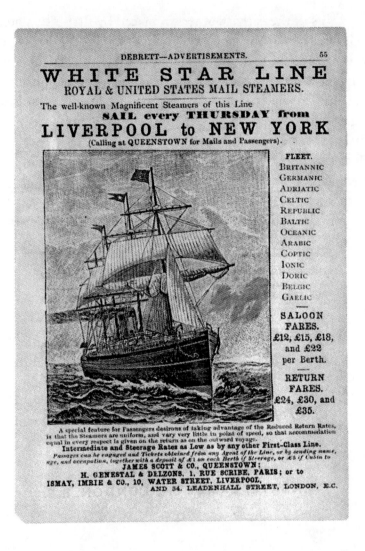

Early White Star Line vessels were propelled by a combination of steam and sail. This White Star Line advertisement from the late 1870's features an illustration of one of the line's boats, names of other ships in the fleet, and passage rates to various ports of call.

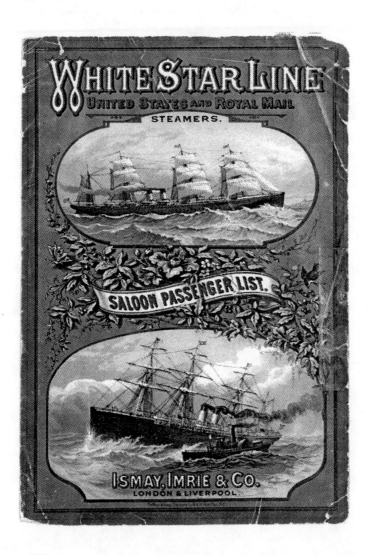

On many of the first transatlantic ocean liners there was only one traveling class known as 'saloon class.' Here, wealthy and immigrant passengers alike shared the same common rooms. This attractive passenger list from the late 1800's for the White Star ship *Britannic* makes mention of Thomas Henry Ismay, founder of the line and also father to Bruce Ismay of later *Titanic* fame.

This canvas White Star Line ticket wallet once held the ticket and assorted immigration papers of a hopeful voyager to the new world. Hoping to attract maximum numbers of immigrant passengers, the White Star Line printed these wallets in Russian, Polish, Swedish, and many other languages.

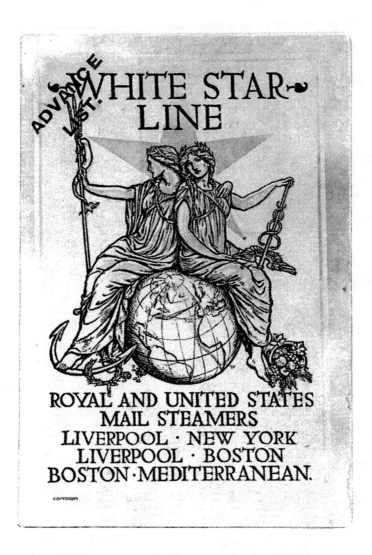

This White Star passenger list is typical of line's commitment at the turn of 20th century to producing aesthetically pleasing printed material which was also often graced with beautiful artwork. Produced for a voyage of the *Adriatic*, this list records the captain for this sailing as E.J. Smith, who would later go on to become master of the infamous *RMS Titanic*.

Titanic.

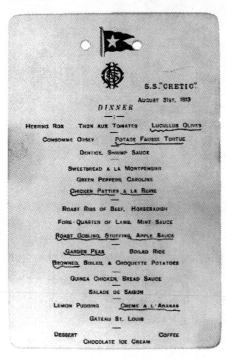

White Star Line officer's cap bearing the now famous red swallow-tail burgee marked with a white star. The buttons on White Star crew members' uniforms also bore an image of the company flag in negative relief.

In sharp contrast to the poor quality of food offered on early ocean liners, this menu for the White Star Line's *Cretic* features extremely fine fare which would have rivaled many leading dining establishments on either side of the Atlantic at the time. Printed for a voyage in 1913, the offerings of this *Cretic* menu were very similar to those enjoyed by the *Titanic's* first class passengers in 1912.

II

A Birth in Belfast *The Olympic*

Under increasing pressure from Cunard and various German steamship lines, White Star was faced with a clear choice—develop new and better ship to meet this challenge, or lose supremacy in the lucrative North Atlantic passenger trade. White Star's answer to the threat was to come on the grandest scale.

While dining with Lord Perrie, managing director of the Harland and Wolff shipyard in Belfast, White Star chairman Bruce Ismay proposed the creation of three massive sister ships. The trio of ships were to be the largest the world had ever seen and were to be built not with speed in mind, but luxury—the sisters would be fitted with the most splendid appointments ever seen in ocean-going vessels. Befitting the glorious hopes for the ships, they would be named the *Olympic*, the *Titanic*, and the *Gigantic* (following the *Titanic* disaster, the latter was changed to the *Britannic*).

The problem confronting Harland and Wolff, however, was how actually to go about building on the scale these new giants demanded. At the firm's Queen's Island yard in Belfast, work was first undertaken to prepare special berths in which to lay down the keels of the new liners, two of which—the *Olympic* and *Titanic*—would begin construction side by side. A massive steel framework known as a gantry was then raised above the berths to facilitate the work which was to follow.

The keel of the *Olympic* was laid down on December 16, 1908 and work began in earnest. Over the following months, the ship's skeleton began to grow and to this framework of steel ribs workers fastened massive hull plates with the aid of hydraulic riveting machines. Slowly, the huge ship began to take shape, towering over the work sheds which dotted the Harland and Wolff property and evoking gasps of awe from all who glimpsed her. She was indeed an olympian achievement.

On October 20, 1910, a huge crowd turned out for the launch of the *Olympic's* now completed hull. At 882 feet in length, *Olympic* was at the time the largest moving object ever made by man, so big that over 22 tons of tallow, soap, and grease were needed to lubricate the ways so that her hull would slide down the slip into the water. Following her launch, *Olympic* was towed over to the fitting-out basin where all of her machinery and internal fittings were added.

Designed to be the last word in ocean-going comfort, *Olympic* was fitted with a salt water swimming pool, a squash court, a gymnasium, and public rooms richly paneled in carved oak, walnut, and mahogany. Propelling the new ship were three massive screws and steam engines that could generate and awesome 55,000 horsepower. To feed the boiler furnaces which provided power to the engines, it would take a staggering 6,000 tons of coal for a one way crossing of the Atlantic Ocean.

The *Olympic* entered service in June 1911 and immediately proved to be very popular with ocean travelers. Although we hear more today of the *Titanic*, it was really the *Olympic* that set the trend in steamship luxury. She was promoted as the "wonder ship of a new age" and indeed she was. But if the public thought that they had seen the last word in ocean liners, they were in for a surprise. The *Olympic's* sister ship was still to be finished and both the White Star Line and Harland and Wolff had a few extras up their sleeves to make this next vessel truly unforgettable.

To accomplish the construction of *Olympic* and *Titanic* (and later *Britannic*), the Belfast ship building firm of Harland and Wolff fashioned a massive steel framework which became known as 'The Great Gantry.' Within this massive structure, *Olympic* and *Titanic* took shape side by side.

Not only was *Olympic* breathtaking when viewed from outside, her interior was similarly awe-inspiring in its workmanship. Skilled master wood carvers created incredible works of art with their hand tools, expressing a dedication to detail all but lost in today's world. This elaborate newel post face from *Olympic's* grand staircase speaks volumes about the talent of the Edwardian carvers. Styled from quarter-cut English white oak, the pattern of this newel face is very similar to one from the *Titanic* found by the victim recovery vessel *Minia*.

This White Star Line promotional booklet bestowed the title of "The Ship Magnificent" on the *Olympic*. Within the pages of the booklet are spectacular photographs of the *Olympic's* interiors which featured, among other elements, passenger elevators and a salt water swimming pool.

This crystal menu holder bearing the White Star Line burgee was purchased on board in *Olympic's* barber shop. On both *Olympic* and *Titanic*, the barber shops carried an assortment of souvenirs which passengers could buy as mementoes of their voyage.

This early postcard of the *Olympic* is typical of the type that was sold on board the ship. Featuring an artist's conception of the vessel, the card hints at the massive scale of the *Olympic's* 45,000 ton hull in comparison with a small sailing boat in the foreground.

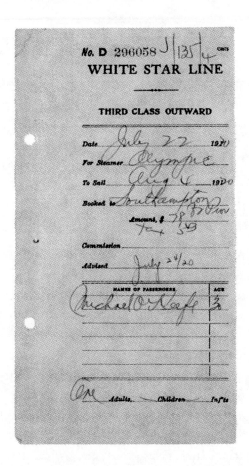

This third class ticket for a trip on the *Olympic* in 1920 is very similar in appearance to those issued for the *Titanic*. The cost of passage on this voyage from New York to Southampton was $78.00 US plus taxes—not a high price by today's standards, but certainly a weighty sum in 1920.

III

Sibling Rivalry *Olympic's sister—Titanic*

Following the launch and fitting out of *Olympic*, the 10,000 plus tradesmen employed at Harland and Wolff turned all of their skills to the completion of her sister, the *Titanic*. And although the public's attention had been focused on the *Olympic*, it was the *Titanic* that was earmarked by White Star to be grander still and the flagship of the fleet.

In outward appearance, sister ships *Olympic* and *Titanic* were quite similar. In much of the pre-voyage promotional literature the two ships are mentioned side by side: "*Olympic* and *Titanic*, the largest and finest steamers in the world." Indeed, the two sisters were, to the lay observer, nearly identical twins with the exception of *Titanic's* first class promenade deck enclosed for half its length in glass windows. This feature was installed so as to protect passengers from salt spray as they strolled.

In features such as these, the builders and owners were capitalizing upon the knowledge acquired from the building and operation of the *Olympic*. However, the addition of the partially enclosed promenade was not the only difference between the sister ships. As construction progressed, White Star seized upon the opportunity to add an additional number of first class suites to the *Titanic*. This addition, in combination with the promenade windows, increased *Titanic's* gross tonnage, and although she was basically the same length as *Olympic*, she could now be considered and promoted as the largest ship in the world by sheer weight alone.

With the construction of the *Olympic* and *Titanic*, Harland and Wolff earned the title of 'complete ship building firm.' That is, they constructed and installed nearly all of the ship's machinery and the adornments for accommodations and public areas. They even built and supplied the 16 regular sized lifeboats of the 20 total which *Titanic* was to carry (the remaining four boats were collapsible with wooden hulls and canvas sides built by another firm.)

Finally, *Titanic's* hull was completed and she was launched on May 31, 1911, before a huge crowd of cheering spectators. Attending the ceremony were an impressive group of dignitaries, although a number of the common rites associated with the launching of a new vessel were absent. There was to be no bottle of champagne broken over *Titanic's* bow before she was released into the water. The lack of ceremony may seem odd, but White Star did not go in for such pomp and circumstance that most believed would bestow good luck on a new ship.

In retrospect, perhaps *Titanic's* creators should have stuck with superstitious routine. However, on the launching day of the giant, it seemed that no such luck was necessary as the event went off without a hitch and the massive hull took to the water mere seconds after the hydraulic triggers were released.

The work was only half completed though, as the *Titanic*, like the *Olympic* before her, had to be towed to a basin where all of her internal fittings and propelling machinery were installed. A massive floating crane, constructed just for such a specialized task, hoisted aboard Titanic's boilers and engine room equipment. At the same time, a beehive of activity invisible to the public's curious eyes was ongoing inside the vessel. Tradesmen of all sorts worked feverishly to prepare *Titanic* for her life at sea; painters applied coats of white paint to public rooms in second and third class areas, carpenters installed hand-carved panels of oak, walnut, and mahogany, and electricians strung miles of cables and wires around the ship.

Gradually the great ship took on a more finished appearance as her huge masts and funnels were raised. Now very near total completion, the great *Titanic's* superstructure and hull were hand-painted by men hanging over her sides in rope slings. Little could anyone dream that just four days into her maiden voyage all of this splendor would vanish from human sight, swallowed whole by the very ocean she had been created to conquer.

This rare 'photo card' of the Great Gantry at the Harland and Wolff shipyard offers a rear view of the sterns of the nearly completed *Olympic*, left, and her sister ship the *Titanic*.

In matters of publicity, both *Olympic* and *Titanic* were usually promoted together. This circa 1910 envelope from the Liverpool head office of the White Star Line features an image of an *Olympic*-class vessel and the caption, "The

Largest Steamers in the World." Below this claim, as if to remind the public that such a feat of engineering could actually be accomplished, appears the simple word, "Building."

A rare promotional pamphlet produced early in 1912 was an example of just one of many styles of booklets issued by White Star to advertise the two revolutionary ships. These unique booklets were commissioned by the White Star Line for distribution to travel agencies that catered to the immigrant and wealthy traveler alike.

The imagination of White Star Line publicists knew no bounds. Prior to the *Olympic* and *Titanic* even having entered service, thousands of these small cards were inserted into tins of Cadbury chocolates. On the front of the card is an image of the *Olympic* or *Titanic* and on the rear is the logo of the chocolate maker. A tin box, also manufactured by Cadbury and featuring the same image, was produced and sold full of the company's chocolates. Once the contents had been consumed, the tin box was designed to hold wooden matches; it even featured a built-in match striker on the underside.

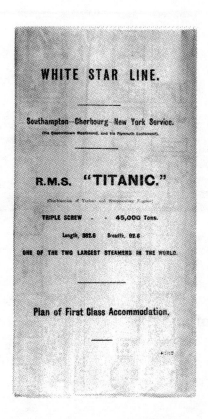

First class passengers, upon booking passage on the *Titanic,* were given a large, fold-out set of deck plans detailing the layout of the first class areas on board. This plan was printed in January of 1912 and was given to a family named ISOM who had booked passage on the *Titanic.* As luck would have it, a member of the family took ill shortly before the voyage and the whole family canceled their *Titanic* reservations.

The Largest and Finest Steamers in the world
WHITE STAR LINE
"OLYMPIC"   ✿   "TITANIC"
882 FEET LONG   45,000 TONS REGISTER   92½ FEET BROAD

On board both the *Olympic* and the *Titanic*, passengers had the
choice of a variety of postcards on sale in the ship barber shops. In most
cases, the cards featured an image of only one ship while making mention of both White Star sisters. This card, circa 1911, is typical of the
cards sold on, and mailed from, the *Titanic*.

This unusual postcard, with postage dated just two days before the *Titanic* sank, features an image of the doomed ship setting sail before a cheering crowd and the huge, superimposed image of an American Bankers Association Travelers Cheque. At the time of the *Titanic's* construction and voyage, the White Star Line was owned by the American

multi-millionaire J.P. Morgan. Morgan also held interests in various banking institutions including the American Bankers Association. This rare postcard is a unique example of a joint promotion between two of Morgan's financial interests.

IV

Four Days to Live *The Titanic at sea*

A short time before the *Titanic's* scheduled maiden voyage, the *Olympic* suffered a collision which required her to be returned to Belfast for repairs. This shift of manpower from the nearly completed *Titanic* to the now damaged *Olympic* delayed the date for the former's premiere excursion. The new date for the *Titanic's* first Atlantic crossing was eventually set for April 10, 1912, departing from Southampton with calls at Cherbourg, France and Queenstown, Ireland.

Following her sea trials, the *Titanic* proceeded to Southampton on April 4, 1912 where she took on supplies, passengers, and crew for her maiden voyage. With only 6 days until departure for New York, the time the *Titanic* spent berthed in Southampton was a virtual flurry of activity. Crates containing hundreds of pieces of china and silverware were unpacked and stowed in the dining areas while in some areas of the ship, workmen were frantically laying carpet and applying final coats of pain. And during all of this, the tons of mail, cargo, and coal the *Titanic* would carry were hoisted aboard by means of her electric deck winches and cranes.

Appointed to command the *Titanic* on the premier trip was White Star's senior captain, Edward John Smith. Nearing the end of his career, Smith was the highest paid transatlantic steamship captain and had taken many of the White star ships out for their maiden voyages. The previous year, Smith commanded the *Olympic* on her first run to New York and legend has it that he planned to retire following the *Titanic's* first voyage.

It must have seemed a relief to Captain Smith when April 10, 1912 arrived and the *Titanic* finally got underway at 12:00 noon. However, Smith was probably not the only person glad to be heading seaward. A number of officers and crew had been transferred over to the *Titanic* from smaller ships laid up because of a coal strike and had been pressed into service on short notice. Now officially on duty, they could finally begin the arduous task of learning to navigate the myriad corridors and decks of the new super-liner.

From Southampton, the *Titanic* steamed on to Cherbourg, France, and Queenstown, Ireland. At both ports of call, tenders brought out additional passengers and hundreds of sacks of mail. It is due to this function of transporting mail across the Atlantic that Titanic bore the prefix 'RMS'—Royal Mail Steamer.

Her passengers and cargo now fully aboard, the *Titanic* weighed anchor and headed away from the Irish coast towards the open Atlantic ocean.

On board were a total of 2228 persons including some of the wealthiest individuals in the world. The first class passenger list boasted such names as Astor, Straus, Guggenheim. Millionaires, business tycoons and wealthy heiresses were all a part of the *Titanic's* elite. But the rich were not the only class of travelers on board. One of the main reasons the *Olympic*-class ships were built so large was so they could accommodate a maximum number of immigrant passengers. Numerous were the impoverished families on the *Titanic* who had their sights set on a fresh start in the New World. Below decks and out of sight from first, second and third class passengers, teams of sweating stokers sang as they shoveled coal into the furnaces of the Titanic's massive boilers. In sharp contrast to the dimly lit and filthy conditions in the stoke holds, first class passengers sat blanketed in deck chairs on the promenade, or sipped tea from fine Spode china in one of the *Titanic's* luxurious public rooms. At dinner time, the *Titanic's* orchestra serenaded wealthy passengers as they descended the grand staircase on their way to dinner.

The days sped by effortlessly and Captain Smith swelled with pride as the *Titanic* covered more and more ocean on her trek to the New World. But as the mammoth ship drew closer and closer to the Labrador current, her radio operators began to receive warnings from other ships ahead. Warnings about ice.

Chosen to command the *Titanic* on her maiden voyage was senior White Star Captain E.J. Smith. This rare picture shows Smith, centre, with his senior officers on board the *Olympic*. The picture was taken in New York upon completion of Olympic's first sailing. A number of men in this picture would later transfer along with Smith over to the *RMS Titanic* and many would perish in the sinking.

Henry Wilde was one of the men who had worked with E.J. Smith on both the *Olympic* and the *Titanic*. On the *Titanic,* he would hold the position of Chief Officer. This picture, taken in the early 1900's, shows Wilde, who is seated at right. Sadly, Wilde would be among those lost in the *Titanic* disaster.

At noon on April 10, 1912, the *Titanic* departed Southampton on her maiden voyage. This scene, clipped from a period newspaper, captures the majesty of the great ship as she headed out to sea.

TITANIC LEAVING SOUTHAMPTON.

This photograph depicts the gigantic vessel being "tugged" out into the open sea

Le « Titanic » en rade de Cherbourg le soir du 10 avril 1912

Collection P. B., Cherbourg

The *Titanic's* first port of call before heading out across the Atlantic was Cherbourg, France. This picture postcard showing the *Titanic* at anchor in Cherbourg harbor was taken at night with the ship's lights blazing across the water. It is a scene eerily similar to what survivors of the sinking would later see from the lifeboats in the early morning hours of April 15, 1912.

The *Titanic* was not only a passenger ship—she was also to transport mail across the Atlantic. This extremely rare letter is stamped and was intended to cross on the *Titanic* in March 1912. Because of a collision suffered by the *Olympic*, the date for *Titanic's* maiden voyage was pushed back to April and this letter made the crossing to America on another vessel.

This White Star Line music list bears an identical cover to those used on board the *Titanic*. Distributed to passengers, the pages of the book list over 300 songs, each identified by a number. In an extraordinary feat of memory, the band on the *Titanic* was able to play any requested title by number alone. Perhaps this is where the phrase, 'Here's a little number,' came from.

Not only was the food in the *Titanic's* first class dining lounge elegant, but so was the tableware. This dinner plate is typical of the service provided first class passengers aboard the *Titanic*.

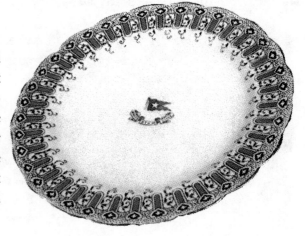

The *Titanic* used generic china patterns which were interchangeable among all ships of the White Star fleet. However, this rare Spode Copeland saucer taken off the *Titanic* before the start of the maiden voyage was an exception to the rule. Even more elegant than the china in first class, this pattern saw exclusive use in *Titanic's* first class A la Carte French-themed restaurant. Pieces of this service were recovered from the wreck site in 1987.

Diners in second class on the *Titanic* also enjoyed fine fare and beautiful table ware in comparison to many other ships in operation during the same era. This dinner plate, made by Minton's China and sporting the White Star Line burgee, is identical to one of the china patterns in use on the *Titanic* in her second class dining lounge.

V

The Final Voyage *Into the Abyss*

It is the evening of April 14, 1912 and the *Titanic* is steaming onward at 21 knots, a speed somewhat shy of her maximum but still a rapid pace considering she is entering a known danger area. During the day of April 14 a number of ships have already wired the *Titanic* to inform her that directly ahead lies a massive ice field filled with hard-packed, towering icebergs. Some of the messages reach the bridge and Captain Smith orders his officers to inform the lookouts to keep a keen watch for icebergs and growler ice.

The time is nearing 20 minutes before midnight. High in *Titanic's* crow's-nest, lookouts Frederick Fleet and Reginald Lee peer out into the moonless night. Although it is a very starry night, the sea is dead calm—conditions Fleet knows will make any iceberg difficult to spot as there will be no foam or lapping waves to reveal its' presence.

Suddenly, Fleet stops what he is saying to Lee in mid-sentence and squints his eyes at the darkness ahead. Acting without hesitation, Fleet rings the crow's-nest bell three times to alert the bridge he has sighted something. His hands trembling and cold he then fumbles in his pocket for the key to the phone-box connecting the lookout perch to the bridge. Seconds pass. In the wind whipped darkness, Fleet struggles to fit the key into the lock. Finally, after what must have seemed an eternity, he succeeds and the door to the phone box flies open. Furiously, Fleet cranks the phone's handle to ring the bridge.[1]

In almost ironic contrast to the frenzied activity in the crow's-nest, a voice on the other end of the line calmly asks what the lookouts have seen. Practically screaming into the mouthpiece, Fleet announces, "Iceberg right ahead!"

Little does anyone yet know, but the *Titanic* is doomed. Despite efforts of the bridge crew to reverse the engines and steer clear of the iceberg, the ship's forward momentum combined with the ineffectiveness of her rudder in full astern mode makes it difficult for the ship to slow, let alone complete a sharp turn. With a grinding shudder, the ship's starboard side collides with the ancient iceberg, showering fragments of ice onto the *Titanic's* forward well deck. Continuing its' progress along the side of the ocean liner, the iceberg does its most gruesome damage below the waterline where it pops off rivet heads and opens up seams between the ship's hull plates. Water begins rushing into the *Titanic's* pierced hull.

Shortly after the collision, Captain Smith asks the *Titanic's* designer, Thomas Andrews, and also her carpenter to sound the ship for damage. The prognosis is grim. The iceberg has caused five of the *Titanic's* sixteen watertight compartments to begin flooding. Too many sections of

---

[1]*Author's note*—The author takes speculative license here when he makes mention of lookout Frederick Fleet using a key to unlock the box which contained the crow's-nest telephone. Although Fleet himself never brought up the issue of using a key to access the telephone, we do know that a lock was fitted to this phone box. One of the keys survives to the present day, having been taken off the *Titanic* by a crew member who did not sail on the maiden voyage. If the crow's-nest telephone was housed in a locked box, and if therefore a key was needed to access the phone, the time taken to open the box may have led to a crucial delay in the transmission of information to the *Titanic's* bridge officers.

the ship are taking on water at once for the pumps to do any good and the increasing weight of seawater in the bow will soon start to pull her down headfirst. Because the watertight bulkheads only extend up as high as E deck, the water flows from one compartment into another as if a giant ice cube tray was being filled. As the *Titanic's* bow dips farther and farther into the sea, Andrews gives the ship about two hours to remain afloat.

Acting on the advice of the designer, Smith orders his officers to begin filling lifeboats with women and children. Due to outdated maritime laws, the *Titanic* carries only enough boats to hold less than a third of her passengers. Their cabins nearest to the boat deck, many first class travelers detect little wrong with the ship and initially refuse to take to the lifeboats. As a result, in the early stages of the disaster, lifeboats designed to hold 65 persons depart with as few as 20 passengers aboard.

Most tragic of all, however, are the conditions further below deck, in third class. Here, passengers can see water on the floor and know something is dreadfully wrong. Terrified, many of them attempt to escape up to the boat decks only to find the way blocked by locked iron gates. In time, a handful of lucky third class passengers manage to make it topside, but by then it is too late and most of the lifeboats have already gone.

During the early stages of the sinking, order is maintained and panic kept to a minimum. However, as the ship tilts higher and higher in its death throes, the situation on deck becomes frantic. The remaining souls on *Titanic's* decks push toward the precious few lifeboats still remaining. Senior officers, issued pistols by the ship's master-at-arms, respond by firing warning shots into the air and along side the hull to stop desperate rushes for the lifeboats. Following the disaster, many newspapers and period publications would report accounts of "cowardly immigrants" actually being gunned down by "brave officers" seeking to protect helpless women and children. Many years later, these reports would be bolstered by a Hampton, New Brunswick undertaker named Thad Stevens who was called to Halifax to work on the bodies of reclaimed *Titanic* victims. Stevens would later claim that John Snow, a Halifax undertaker, had personally told him that he had seen evidence of gunshot wounds on the bodies of some of the recovered victims.

While the situation on the boat deck of the *Titanic* deteriorates, the Marconi wireless radio operators stick steadfastly to their posts in hopes of being able to contact a ship near enough to assist. Their efforts prove to be in vain and just before 2:20 a.m. on the morning of April 15, the *Titanic's* stern rises upwards, "pointing like a finger towards heaven." Having rowed their lifeboats well clear of the *Titanic* fearing being sucked underwater by whirlpool suction during the imminent sinking, survivors hear a deafening series of noises from within the ship as everything unattached slides toward her submerged bow. Some of the survivors would later go on to claim they had heard a number of massive explosions from inside the ship which could possibly have been the last lit boilers exploding upon contact with the ice cold sea water. Whatever the source of the rumbling noise, it was soon followed by an even greater din as the *Titanic* broke in half between her third and fourth funnels and her stern smashed down on the water, crushing many of the swimmers struggling for their lives.

Out of sight well below the waterline, the *Titanic's* bow detaches from the stern and begins the long voyage to the bottom, some two miles below. On the still buoyant stern section, hundreds of remaining passengers cling in terror to the railings or anything else available on deck and pray for a miracle. It was divine intervention that would never come. Only moments after the *Titanic* had broken in two, the stern tilts up, revolves, and sinks into the ocean's murky depths.

For the hundreds of souls who survive the sinking, the fierce battle for life continues versus the lethal effects of hypothermia. It is a fight that most of the men, women and children have no chance of winning.

As survivors in the lifeboats weep and listen, the screams from across the sea die out and are replaced by a far more ominous sound—the sound of silence.

MORE DEVASTATING THAN THE SWORD: THE WEAPON OF THE ICE KING.

As early as 1909, newspapers and periodicals were featuring articles on the dangers of icebergs to commercial and passenger shipping. This article, from the *London Illustrated News* of January 2, 1909, was accompanied by the photograph of a massive iceberg and the chilling caption, "More devastating than the sword: The weapon of the ice king." For the *Titanic*, these ominous words would prove all too true.

Frantic attempts to steer the *Titanic* away from the oncoming wall of ice failed, and mere moments after the order had been given to turn the helm 'hard over' the iceberg ripped a lethal tear into the starboard side of the *Titanic's* bow. For many years, the precise damage exacted by the iceberg was a bone of contention among researchers of the disaster. Some believed the collision had torn a huge gash in the *Titanic's* side while others argued that the berg scraped along the side and punched in a number of hull plates.

In the early 1990's, a new theory emerged which named brittle steel hull-plates as the main culprit leading to the flooding which doomed the *Titanic*. One popular scientific magazine even theorized that due to brittle metal, the ship's hull-plates may have "shattered like glass," upon striking the iceberg.

This fascinating photograph, taken following the collision of the White Star ship *Doric* with another vessel in the mid-1930's, effectively argues against the 'brittle hull' theory and points to a more likely scenario. The view, taken from the *Doric's* wing bridge, shows a massive hull plate bent inwards and missing an entire double row of rivets (left). To the right of the gash, there is a piece of the hull frame with rivet heads gone and mere rivet stems remaining. This sort of damage is typical to what any riveted-hull ship would suffer in a collision regardless of the brittleness of hull plates.

In the *Titanic's* case, the iceberg pushed in the hull plates and force was transferred to their edges, where the plates were fastened, causing the rivet heads to pop off. Seams then opened up between the hull plates allowing the entry of water.

In the last few years, a new theory has been put forward which focuses on the rivets themselves as major contributors to the sinking. Testing of rivets raised from the *Titanic* wreck has shown they are high in slag content and therefore brittle. In the testing of such materials as hull metal and rivets, perhaps researchers are neglecting the basic fact that inferior materials are not the exclusive cause of maritime sinkings. Put simply, ocean liners before the *Titanic* and since are simply not designed to collide with objects such as icebergs and emerge unscathed.

SINKING OF THE STEAMSHIP TITANIC, WITH A LOSS OF 1,635 HUMAN LIVES.
Scenes After the Collision of the Great Vessel With the Iceberg, While the Lifeboats Were Pulling Away From Her Sides, as Drawn From Descriptions of Survivors.

This illustration, from an unknown 1912 newspaper, depicts the *Titanic* in the early stages of the disaster. Since the in rushing water was below decks and out of sight from most passengers, many were reluctant to forego the warmth of the ship to board a cold, uncovered lifeboat. As a result of this initial reluctance, one of the first lifeboats to depart from the *Titanic* left with only 20 persons aboard despite having a capacity of 65.

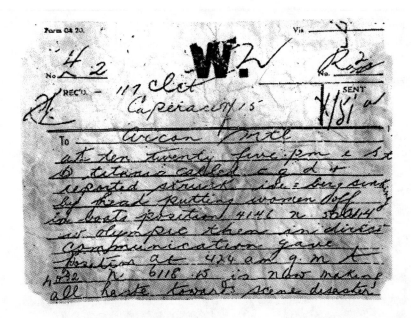

This wireless radio message, transmitted via Cape Race, Newfoundland to Montreal, Quebec, conveys a very real sense of the dramatic events unfolding on the *Titanic* in the mid-Atlantic during the early morning hours of April 15, 1912. Particularly striking are the words, "sinking by the head, putting women off in boats."

As the *Titanic* lay sinking, her Marconi radio operators tried frantically to summon assistance. This picture, taken in the wireless 'shack' on board the Olympic, shows the same type of radio equipment that was used on board the *Titanic*.

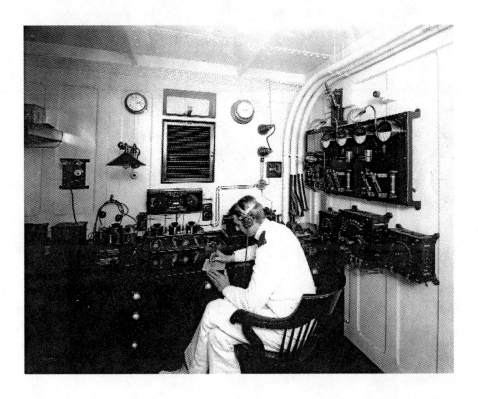

Despite the panic and fear on the decks of the sinking *Titanic*, many moving acts of bravery and compassion took place. Pictured above, wealthy Jewish couple Ida and Isidor Straus were returning home to New York on board the *Titanic*. As husband Isidor was a partner in the successful and popular Macy's department store, the couple were among the doomed ship's most prosperous first class passengers. An elderly gentleman, Isidor was offered a precious place aboard one of the lifeboats. He declined, however, declaring that he would not go before any of the other, younger men were to be evacuated. He then proceeded to assist his wife Ida and their maid into one of the boats and stepped back to await his fate. In an incredible act of courage, Ida Straus stepped off of the lifeboat and returned to the side of the man she loved. Survivors later claimed to have overheard Ida say to her husband, "We have been together for many years. Where you go, I go." The couple then seated themselves in folding deck chairs, took each other's hand, and waited for the end. Both Ida and Isidor Straus perished in the sinking of the *RMS Titanic.*

This memorial postcard, printed just after the disaster, presents a fairly accurate view of the position the *Titanic's* stern maintained in the final moments of the sinking. As the bow section of the Titanic flooded and sank further into the sea, her stern tilted high into the night, pointing, as one survivor later described, "like a finger toward heaven."

Shortly before 2:20 am on the morning of April 15, 1912, a thunderous noise boomed out across the sea as the *Titanic's* straining hull broke apart between her third and fourth funnels. Now completely detached from the stern section, the bow plunged downward into the abyss. In mere moments, the stern was deluged and also began the long descent to the bottom. As the two sections fell, thousands of objects from within the torn hull rained down onto the sea floor. In dives to the *Titanic* in 1987, items identical to this ladle, third class soup bowl, toothpaste jar lid, and smoking room floor tile were sighted among, and in some cases recovered from, the extensive debris field.

VI

The Lucky *Carpathia*

As the *Titanic* laid sinking, her wireless operators frantically sent out calls for assistance to any and all ships within range. Both CQD and SOS blast out across the North Atlantic Ocean and are received by a number of vessels at sea that night. Unfortunately, all of the ships hearing the *Titanic's* cries for help are too far away to assist. However, one ship, the Cunard Line's *Carpathia*, received the distress calls and sped to the rescue. The *Carpathia* is a smaller, single funnel ship which was outward bound from New York on a cruise to the Mediterranean.

On receiving the call for assistance from the *Titanic*, the *Carpathia's* captain Arthur Rostron ordered his ship to turn north and proceed at full speed to the imperiled ship's position. To maximize his ship's speed, Rostron ordered steam heating and hot water to the cabins shut off so the engines could utilize every last bit of steam pressure. Not only did Rostron order full speed, he also ordered the *Carpathia* readied for the reception of survivors. Lounges were transformed into virtual hospital wards, lines were let down the sides of the ship, and canvas bags were readied to hoist aboard any children or injured survivors. Rostron even had some of his crew wind heavy coils of rope around sturdy deck chairs in case they were actually faced with binding and restraining any survivors driven mad by the disaster. Making Rostron's journey all the more hazardous were the ever thickening ice fields being encountered on the race northward. Without the captain's seagoing skill, the *Carpathia* could very well have met the same fate as the *Titanic*.

Finally, just as the sun was beginning to rise on the morning of April 15, 1912, Carpathia reached the site of the *Titanic's* demise. As the officers on the Cunard Line ship's bridge watched in disbelief, a number of the *Titanic's* lifeboats became visible among the floating chunks of ice. One by one the boats pulled alongside the *Carpathia* and the dazed survivors were helped aboard. Once all of the lifeboats had been cleared and all were safely aboard, Carpathia steamed toward America. Rescued were just 705 passengers out of a total 2,228 people who had been aboard the doomed *Titanic*.

On her way to New York, very little information was given out by the *Carpathia's* wireless operator as to the details of the sinking. The media criticized this blackout and rumors ran wild in the press about the disaster. One newspaper even reported that the *Titanic* was only slightly damaged by the iceberg and was being towed to Halifax for repairs.

On the evening of April 18, 1912, Carpathia finally arrived at New York. As thousands of spectators looked on, survivors disembarked and the *Titanic's* now empty lifeboats were unloaded. For his role in the rescue, Captain Rostron was hailed as a hero and would eventually rise through the ranks to become commodore of the Cunard fleet. Sadly, the *Carpathia*, the gallant little ship who rescued the survivors of the *Titanic*, came to rest on the bottom of the same ocean she had once raced across on her brave recovery mission thanks to a German torpedo in the First World War.

The *Carpathia*, a small single-funneled vessel of Cunard fleet, was over 50 miles away from the disaster and on her way to the Mediterranean when she first picked up the *Titanic's* desperate radio calls for assistance. Of all the ships at sea that night, the *Carpathia* was the only one to respond in time to rescue the 705 survivors in the *Titanic's* lifeboats.

Upon hearing news of the *Titanic's* peril, the *Carpathia's* captain, Arthur Rostron, ordered his ship to head north at full speed toward the foundering ship's position. He even ordered that all steam heating and hot water to passenger cabins be cut so that the *Carpathia's* engines could use every bit of available steam. For his brave actions, Rostron was hailed as a hero and knighted. In time, he ascended through the ranks of the Cunard Line to become commodore of the fleet.

A passenger's boarding pass from the Cunard Line ship, *Carpathia.*

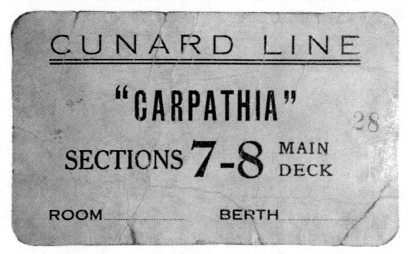

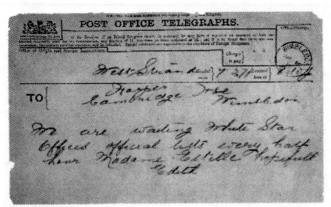

In Wimbledon, the wife of a first class passenger on board the *Titanic*, W.T. Stead, anxiously awaited news as to his fate. This telegram, sent by the Steads' maid, Edith, reads: "We are waiting White Star offices, official lists every half hour, Madame Estelle hopeful. Edith."

Back in Southampton, as news filtered in from overseas, the White Star Line erected a massive bulletin board illuminated by electric lights. In this rare photograph, one can discern the lists of the passengers saved or lost which have been posted on the board.

After the *Carpathia* rescued the *Titanic's* survivors and hoisted its 13 lifeboats aboard, she steamed onward to New York. During the entire voyage, the *Carpathia's* radio man, Harold Cottam, and the surviving junior wireless operator from the

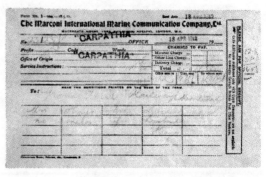

Titanic, Harold Bride, sent numerous messages to shore stations detailing the names of those saved from the wreck and those lost. This telegram form, the original from the *Carpathia*, carries a message dispatched from the widow of Grand Trunk Pacific Railway president Charles M. Hays to the head office of the railway in Montreal, Canada. Touching in its simplicity, the telegram reads: "Mrs. Hays, Mrs. Davidson

safe. No news of husbands. Hays." The initials of the operator who sent the telegram are marked on the form, and are those of Harold Bride, the *Titanic's* surviving Marconi man.

Refusing to answer radio inquiries from journalists, the *Carpathia's* radio operator Harold Cottam instead concentrated on sending massages informing who had been lost and who saved from the *Titanic* shipwreck. This information blackout forced many newspapers to go to press running speculative accounts as to the *Titanic's* fate. This newspaper front page, from the *Los Angeles Evening Herald* of April 15, 1912, reported that all of the *Titanic's* passengers had been saved by the liner *Virginian*.

When the *Carpathia* reached New York, she first unloaded the *Titanic's* 13 lifeboats which had been recovered from the sea on the rescue mission. The boats were corralled into a group and guarded through the night by dock workers and New York City police officers. Despite this tight protection, enterprising souvenir hunters nonetheless managed to remove a number of the cast nameplates and flag pennants from the lifeboats' bows. This cast brass flag, in the shape of a White Star Line pennant, is believed to be one of those removed from the lifeboats held in New York.

VII

The Lost *The search for the Titanic's dead*

In the days following the *Titanic's* loss, other ships traveling the transatlantic route began to radio that they had sighted huge fields of floating debris and bodies. In response to this information, and to satisfy relatives' desires to claim and bury the bodies of lost family members, the White Star Line chartered a series of vessels to begin recovery missions. The first two of four vessels ultimately sent to the disaster area were the transatlantic cable ships the *Mackay-Bennett* and the *Minia*. These vessels laid submarine telegraph cable and were chosen for the operation in part because of their familiarity with the area of the North Atlantic in which the *Titanic* had foundered.

On April 17, 1912, the cable ship *Mackay-Bennett* steamed out of Halifax harbor and headed north towards the disaster area. On board, she carried hundreds of crude wooden coffins, embalmers and their supplies, and tons of ice in her hold in which to pack bodies. Also on board were clergy members who would say prayers over any recovered bodies. Canvas bags and iron bars were also carried should it become necessary to bury victims at sea.

Using coordinates passed on to her by other ships which had sighted wreckage and bodies, the *Mackay-Bennett* arrived on location and began the gruesome work. Victims' bodies, most wearing white, cork-filled,

Fosbery brand life jackets, were pulled aboard lifeboats which had been lowered from the salvage ship. One by one the corpses were brought on board the cable steamer where the contents of pockets and other personal effects were examined in attempts to establish positive identities. During the course of the examinations, each body was numbered, tagged, and any personal effects placed into canvas bags marked with number corresponding to the remains. Depending on the class of the passenger and condition of the body, the dead were either embalmed and placed in coffins (coffins were reserved for first class passengers), embalmed and packed in ice, or shrouded in weighted canvas wraps and returned to the sea.

After days of grueling work, the *Mackay-Bennett* had recovered some 306 bodies, 116 of which were buried at sea. While on site, the ship also salvaged a quantity of flotsam from the *Titanic*. Eager for souvenirs of the epic event, *Mackay-Bennett* crewmen retrieved and kept numerous pieces of woodwork, deck chairs, and even life jackets removed from the recovered dead.

Her embalming supplies running low, the *Mackay-Bennett* was relieved on April 26, 1912 by the cable ship *Minia*. After a week's search, the *Minia's* crew had succeeded in recovering just 17 victims, including Charles M. Hays, president of Canada's Grand Trunk Pacific Railway. Ultimately, due to rough weather and the ever broadening field of victims, the *Minia* abandoned her search and returned to Halifax, arriving on May 6, 1912. Like the *Mackay-Bennet* before her, the *Minia* also recovered quantities of wreck wood, deck chairs, and life jackets. At least two of her crew members—William Parker and Bertram King—would go on to fashion some of the recovered woodwork into usable objects such as picture frames and even large items of household furniture.

As a last ditch effort to recover any remaining bodies, two more ships—the *Montmagny* and the *Algerine*—were dispatched to the area of the catastrophe. By this point, owing to the passage of time and the

effect of ocean currents, the two ships recovered a mere handful of victims between them before the entire recovery operation was suspended.

Back in Halifax, many of the dead brought ashore were prepared by
undertakers and laid out in the city's Mayflower Curling Rink. In the
solemn privacy of this makeshift morgue, visiting relations and family
friends attempted to identify victims prior to their being shipped
home for burial. The remaining bodies—just over 150 unclaimed or
unidentified—were laid to rest in three Halifax cemeteries. In this
final destination, rows of black headstones bearing the date of April
15, 1912 offer up silent yet moving testimony to the tragic toll of the
RMS Titanic.

The first vessel chartered by the White Star Line to search for victims of the *Titanic* sinking was the cable steamer *Mackay-Bennett.* This Halifax newspaper from April 30, 1912 reported on the recovery ship's return to port and the subsequent removal of victims to the makeshift morgue set up in the city's Mayflower Curling Rink.

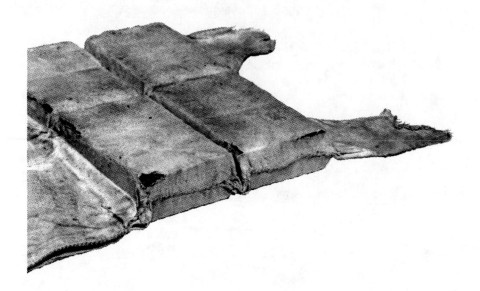

Most of the bodies found by the recovery ships were clad in white, cork-filled life jackets. The vests kept people afloat and prevented drowning, but they did little to offset the deadly effects of the ice cold Atlantic water. Pictured is a damaged panel from a cork-filled life jacket which was found in the Canadian Maritimes. The damaged vest matches the specifications and appearance of the Fosbery life jackets worn by recovered victims from the *Titanic*.

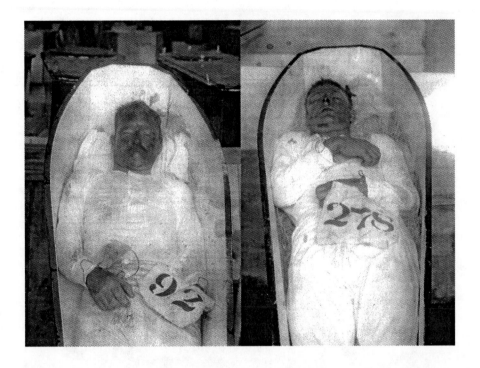

Once bodies were brought aboard recovery ships, they were issued numbered tags and their physical characteristics were recorded to assist with the identification process. These two bodies, numbers 92 and 278, remained unidentified. The coroner's notation on the back of one of these photos speculated that one of the men was "possibly a fireman." These two photographs were taken at Halifax's Mayflower Curling Rink where bodies were displayed for possible identification by visiting relatives or acquaintances. Resting on each of the bodies in the photographs are canvas bags, each bearing a number matching that which was assigned the corresponding physical remains. It was into these sacks that any personal effects which accompanied the bodies were placed.

This pocket watch, found on the body of an unidentified victim from the *Titanic*, clearly shows the effects of exposure to salt water in addition to damage suffered during the sinking.

In addition to bodies, the recovery ships also brought aboard quantities of floating surface wreckage. This piece of carved English Oak was found by the cable ship *Minia*. A study of the *Titanic's* interior reveals that this carving pattern matches a decorative border which ran under the handrail of both the fore and aft first class grand staircases of the *Titanic*. This particular section bears the number, "9303," and the word, "aft," indicating that this piece of wood was once part of the ship's rearmost grand staircase.

Another intricately carved section of oak found by recovery ships was this small piece of decorative molding. Inscribed with a distinct leaf and berry pattern, the length of wood matches similar molding which appears in photographs of the first class Louis XIV suite on board the *Olympic*. As the *Titanic* and the *Olympic* were sister ships, they shared near identical fittings and stateroom themes. A number of historians believe that the Louis XIV suite on the *Titanic* was occupied by John Jacob Astor, the wealthiest passenger on the voyage.

Floating amid the fields of detritus and corpses were hundreds of wooden, folding deck chairs bearing the carved star emblem of the White Star Line on their head rests. During the *Titanic's* sailing, many passengers rested in the lap of luxury on the deck in these same chairs. After the ship's sinking, the chairs were pressed into a very different sort of service as passengers clung for their lives to them, using them as life-rafts to keep afloat above the deadly, freezing water. This particular deck chair is one of an unknown quantity salvaged by the crews of recovery ships from the *Titanic's* disaster area. In turn, many were taken home by crew members to be put to use on porches and lawns.

In some cases, objects significantly larger than deck chairs were hauled on board salvage ships and kept as souvenirs. Oral history reports that this trunk was brought aboard the *Mackay-Bennett* only to later find its way to the home of a New Brunswick minister.

The second ship sent to participate in the recovery missions was the cable steamer *Minia*. This photograph shows the *Minia* in Halifax harbor in the late 19th century. In 1912, by the time of the *Titanic* recovery mission, the cable steamer's hull color had been changed from black to white.

James Adams was the *Minia's* chief officer at the time of the *Titanic* disaster in 1912. Like many of his fellow crew men, Adams salvaged and kept a number of mementoes of the tragedy. This photograph was taken early in Adams's career on the *Minia* and dates back to the late 19th century.

In one of the only known photos of the *Minia's* chart room, her chief officer, James Adams, strikes a contemplative pose while gazing seaward. Little could Adams have known that just a few short years later he would peer out the same window upon a sea littered with the wreckage and victims of the 'unsinkable' *Titanic.*

The *Minia's* carpenter, William Parker, found a practical use for the quantity of wreck-wood from the *Titanic* recovered by his ship mates. Rather than leave the wood in its salvage state, Parker put his resourceful mind and hands to work and constructed useful objects from the wreckage. Among Parker's creations were picture frames, document boxes, and game boards. In what can perhaps be considered the 'masterpiece' of his projects, Parker crafted the bedside table illustrated above. Inlaid in the tabletop are numerous sections of oak, walnut, and mahogany. To date, this is the largest object known to have been constructed of wooden wreckage retrieved from the wreck of the *Titanic*.

A number of the victim recovery ships utilized partial volunteer crews for the gruesome work of body retrieval. Bertram King, pictured, was a Halifax seaman who is believed to have served in this capacity on the *Minia's* mission to the *Titanic* disaster area.

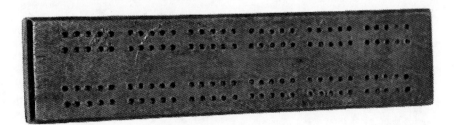

Bertram King, like the *Minia's* carpenter and others, also saw a use for recovered wooden detritus from the *Titanic*. He went on to fashion a cribbage board from a piece of mahogany recovered by the *Minia*.

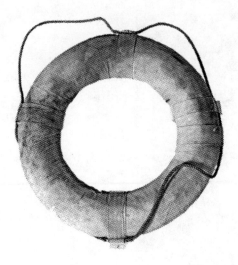

One of the most remarkable objects to be fished from the sea was this *Titanic* life ring. Believed to have been found during the recovery mission of the *Algerine* (the last ship to take part in the search for victims), the life ring bears a British Board of Trade inspector's stamp dated April 6, 1912. The stamp would have been applied while the *Titanic* was docked at Southampton taking on supplies for her maiden voyage.

VIII

A Mighty Wake *The world's reaction*

As the initial shock of the *Titanic's* loss faded, new emotions of sorrow and grief tugged at the world's heartstrings. It was not long before these sentiments gave way to anger and rage as the public and media at large began to demand answers as to how such a disaster could have occurred. In Washington, a senate inquiry was convened and many of the *Titanic's* surviving crew members were detained to provide testimony at the official proceedings.

In many ways, being held in America came as a severe hardship to many of the surviving crew members. Many of them, from common stewards to ranking officers, had lost everything in the sinking. Adding to this discomfort was the fact that there was no relief pay forthcoming. In the *Titanic's* day, the loss of one's ship meant a loss of pay, which effectively ended the moment a vessel foundered. Acting out of compassion, a number of U.S. charity organizations were moved to alleviate the crew's plight and soon the men were offered everything from fresh changes of clothing to olive tree branches to sell on street corners for much needed pocket change.

The forced poverty of many of these men translated into an agonizing wait for news back home in the United Kingdom. Without the funds to send a telegram to loved ones overseas, the crewmen's wives and relations were forced to sit through many cruel days unsure as to whether their husbands or fathers had actually been saved from the wreck. In fact, there were even cases of notification announcing the supposed death of seamen delivered to some of these families when the victim in question was actually alive and well in America. It was indeed a difficult time for all involved.

The U.S. Senate investigation into the causes of the *R.M.S. Titanic* disaster got underway on April 19, 1912. Over the course of seventeen days, hundreds of pages of testimony were taken from surviving Titanic crew members and passengers in an attempt to find the causes of the sinking and ensure that such a tragedy never take place again.

Conducted in a formal and dignified manner, the senate inquiry stood in sharp contrast to the yellow journalism which appeared daily in bold headlines across the pages of the nation's many newspapers. Journalists eager to satisfy the public's calls for a scapegoat targeted survivor of the *Titanic* and chairman of the White Star Line J. Bruce Ismay and the master of the Leyland liner *Californian*, Captain Stanley Lord. Branded a coward, Ismay's crime apparently was to have survived at all when women and children had perished. If the public believed that the captain of a ship should go down with his vessel, they seemed to feel that the rule should similarly apply to the chairman of line which owned the sinking ship. Had anyone used common sense, they would have realized that there was no need to punish Ismay. Watching his flagship sink on her maiden voyage and being forced to sit helpless listening to the cries of the dying was certainly damnation enough.

If the criminalization of Bruce Ismay seemed harsh, it was nothing compared to what Captain Stanley Lord was forced to endure. As the *Titanic* foundered, Lord's ship was roughly 14 miles away and had stopped for the night on account of the massive ice field in their path. Lord had turned in for the night and was sound asleep in his cabin when his bridge officers reported to him that they had sighted a series of white rockets exploding in the distance. He responded to this news by telling his officers to try to raise whoever was firing the rockets with a small signal lamp known as a Morse lamp. Lord might as well have done nothing at all, because, at the range of 14 miles, the lamp was useless. If Lord had ordered his Marconi operator to power up his set (it was not mandatory in 1912 for radio operators to man their sets 24 hours a day) he would have heard in loud, blasting signals what was taking place. The charge of failing to assist a vessel in distress haunted Lord for the remainder of his life and numerous attempts by both himself and others to clear his name have proved largely unsuccessful. Although it may be true, as was later claimed, that there were other ships in the immediate vicinity of the sinking *Titanic*, the fact that Lord's watch officers saw white rockets and reported them to their captain cannot be refuted. And rockets at sea, then as now, mean only one thing—distress.

The U.S. Senate hearing wrapped up on May 25, 1912. The final result of the inquiry was a condemnation of the high speed at which the *Titanic* was traveling in a known danger area (although she was not at full speed) and a number of sweeping recommendations to improve the safety of seagoing vessels. Among the suggestions were; increased numbers of lifeboats with enough space for every passenger on board, the formation of the International Ice Patrol to monitor the movements of icebergs in the North Atlantic, and that Marconi radio sets be manned 24 hours a day. Regretfully, as wise and noble as these planned revisions were, they came too late to help the 1,523 victims of the *Titanic*. True to human nature, it had taken the senseless loss of life to bring about safety regulations which should have existed all along.

Many people around the globe were moved by the loss of the *Titanic*. This letter, written in April 1912, provides a glimpse into the way many at the time viewed the disaster. Mailed by a nun in Scotland to a woman in Halifax, Nova Scotia, the tone of the letter

bears a distinctly moralistic tone. In part it reads:

"All thought of the present, and none of the future. As a clever priest here said, nothing but love making, feasting, and dressing from morning till night. I expect you will see some of the victims at Halifax. Poor, wretched creatures. Men liken to think themselves gods, but they soon have their eyes opened."

> Butt on deck waving his cap and smiling. He was engaged to be married to a miss Williams of some northern city. John Jacob Astor was lately married and they (he and his wife) were returning from a cruise in the Mediterranean. He told his wife "good-bye" and went down with the others. I believe I would go crazy or die one, when I thought about the bodies of any of my people floating around in the sea, or, perhaps, being swallowed by sharks. If I had been a passenger on that ship, and had been sent away in a life boat I should have died or, at least, fainted to go away and leave people on board to sink. I could hardly have left the place safe unless all could have done it, too.

Another 1912 letter, this one written by a young woman to the man courting her, displays a rather different perspective. In this note, the writer tries to imagine how she would have reacted had she been aboard the doomed *Titanic*.

Parish Church of Liverpool.

MEMORIAL SERVICE

FOR

The Victims of the "Titanic" Disaster.

SATURDAY, APRIL 20th, 1912.

ORGAN VOLUNTARY—"FUNERAL MARCH."—*Chopin.*

THE SERVICE WILL FOLLOW

ORDER FOR THE BURIAL OF THE DEAD.

The opening sentences will be sung.

I AM the resurrection and the life, saith the Lord; he that believeth in me, though he were dead, yet shall he live; and whosoever liveth and believeth in me shall never die.—*St. John* xi. 25, 26.

I KNOW that my Redeemer liveth, and that he shall stand at the latter day upon the earth. And though after my skin worms destroy this body, yet in my flesh shall I see God; whom I shall see for myself, and mine eyes shall behold and not another.—*Job* xix. 25, 26, 27.

WE brought nothing into this world, and it is certain we can carry nothing out. The Lord gave, and the Lord hath taken away; blessed be the name of the Lord.

1 *Tim.* vi. 7.   *Job* i. 21.

Around the world, memorial services were held for the victims of the disaster. Of note was this particular ceremony held in Liverpool, England, the *Titanic's* home port.

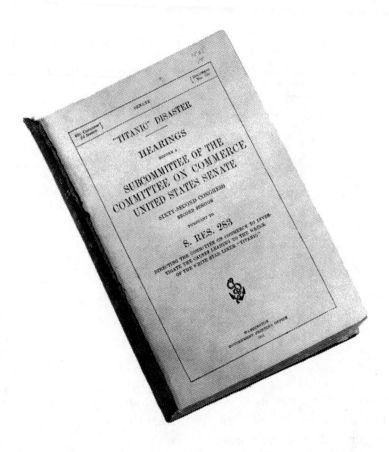

Sparked by the massive loss of life on the *Titanic*, the public at large and politicians demanded answers as to how such a disaster could have occurred. In both the United States and Britain, official government inquiries were convened to probe for the possible causes of the sinking. This hardbound volume contains all testimony presented at the US Senate inquest into the loss of the *RMS Titanic*.

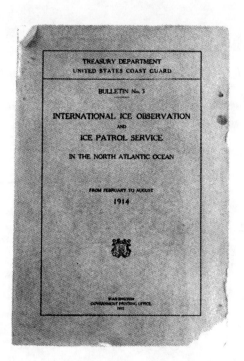

One of the recommendations of the US Senate inquiry was the formation of a service to monitor the movement of icebergs in relation to
commercial and passenger shipping lanes. The newly formed organiza-
tion was known as the International Ice Patrol. Every year the patrol
published a softbound volume detailing the movements of icebergs and
the general hydrographic conditions in the North Atlantic.

Following the completion of the US Senate inquiry, many of the survivors from the *Titanic's* crew were sent home to the United Kingdom on board the above pictured Red Star Line vessel, the *Lapland.*

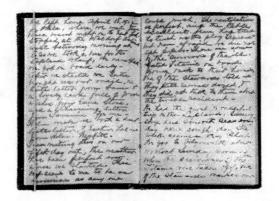

This diary, kept by a young woman traveling on the *Lapland,* mentions the surviving crew members from the *Titanic* who were aboard the ship. She wrote: "There are some of the survivors of the ill-fated *Titanic* on board going back to their homes. One of the stewards (of the *Lapland*) told us they still seemed dazed and they did not talk to them about the terrible accident."

This photograph was taken on board the *Lapland* during the voyage to return surviving *Titanic* crew members to their homes in the United Kingdom.

In its May 1, 1912 edition, the British news magazine *Bystander* recorded the arrival at Plymouth of the *Lapland* and the *Titanic* survivors it carried.

For the survivors of the *Titanic*, there remained the task of trying to return to a normal life. Many were haunted by the doomed ship until the day they died. This letter, written to *Titanic* survivor Lillian Bentham in May 1912, offered the opinion that the ocean liner may become a lifelong companion: "Dear Lillian, you certainly can never forget (the *Titanic*) as long as you live…"

IX

Tribute and Trinkets *Titanic memorialized*

Following the search for answers in the two official inquiries and the character assassination of the perceived villains of the *Titanic* disaster, the world set about to pay homage to the heroes of the disaster. Arthur Rostron, master of the *Carpathia*, was presented with a silver loving cup by *Titanic* survivor 'Unsinkable' Molly Brown as a token of appreciation from all of the survivors of the disaster. Likewise, Rostron's crew each received medals for the part they had played in the rescue. In the U.K., a huge crowd turned out for the funeral of the *Titanic's* bandmaster Wallace Hartley. A stone monument capped with a bust of Hartley was commissioned to immortalize his and his band's bravery and dedication in playing their instruments until ship's the bitter end. To honor the engineers who had stayed at their posts to maintain the power flowing to *Titanic's* lights and radio system, a huge monument was constructed in Southampton, the ship's port of departure.

Over time, a number of other monuments, statues, and plaques appeared, paying homage to everyone from Ida and Isidor Straus to the *Titanic's* infamous captain, E.J. Smith. For the survivors themselves, tributes often took the form of letters of thanks to both one another and to those of the rescue teams. In some cases, personal gifts acknowledging individual acts of kindness towards survivors would prove to be lifelong keepsakes to rescuers.

The world mourned collectively and thoughts of the disaster played strongly on the minds of millions. Cashing in on this sudden surge of interest in the *Titanic*, entrepreneurs began to crank out a number of mass produced items, each of which was designed to turn the public's need to memorialize the great disaster into cold, hard cash. The most common of these products were numerous postcards, usually featuring an image of the ship (in most cases not even the *Titanic*, but some other four-funneled liner) and listing details of the sinking such as the number of lives lost and other facts. Also produced were tissue place-mats, posters and prints, and numerous pieces of sheet music which sought to bring the disaster to life through song.

Memorial books, each claiming to contain 'thrilling true stories of survivors' were peddled door to door by traveling salesmen. Although a number of these books had different colored covers and slightly different titles, they were in many cases the same book rebound and common was the case of someone purchasing three or four versions of the identical book. Although these volumes claimed to tell real accounts from actual survivors, in most cases the information was far from truthful. Eager to reap profit from the *Titanic* tragedy, many fly-by-night publishers scoured period newspaper accounts of the disaster for articles that were often reproduced verbatim, without any verification of factual content.

It is partly due to what these books supposedly revealed that many myths about the *Titanic's* sole voyage began not only to circulate, but also to sink into the public's consciousness for generations to come. Many of the falsehoods were given lasting life; that the ship was trying to set a speed record during her crossing, that officers claimed the *Titanic* to be unsinkable, and even that Captain Smith had committed suicide with a pistol as the ship went down.

To the public at large, the issue of accuracy did not really seem to matter and they snapped up thousands of the memorial books as well as countless other items. It was as if people needed to connect themselves to the disaster, even if only at a distance. In many respects, people have changed little since 1912 as the phenomenon of needing to own an object to feel a connection to an important event continues to exist.

There were some who had every right to desire a tangible souvenir of the *Titanic*. At the Harland and Wolff shipyard in Belfast, where over 10,000 men had labored to build the great ship, some workers took home rivets left over from construction and stamped the words 'S.S. *Titanic*, April 15th, 1912' into the rivet heads. In the same way a grieving relation holds on to a personal effect from a departed loved one, so the men of Harland and Wolff strove to remember and pay tribute to their greatest creation. To them, the *Titanic* was like a lost child who did not live long enough past birth to realize her true potential.

During her own era and well into our own, the *Titanic* has become many things to many people—a reminder of a simpler time and place, an icon of an age unequaled in opulence, or a massive money-making machine. Too often we forget that the *Titanic* was much more than these few superficial things. Rather, the *Titanic's* fate remains a potent lesson, a cautionary tale steeped in the human traits of greed, hubris, and the misguided belief that technology will naturally breed a safer world and keep humanity from harm. Technology may change, but human nature does not. Undoubtedly, there will be many more April-fifteenths for mankind, although the iceberg may not be a wall of hard-packed ice but perhaps something still more menacing and nebulous.

If we as a species hope to stand any chance of avoiding such disasters, we must learn from what the *Titanic* can still teach us—the wisdom of reducing speed, casting aside arrogance, and proceeding with extreme caution.

THE ILL-FATED S. S. TITANIC. FOUNDERED APRIL 15, 1912.

It was not long after the sinking that numerous memorial postcards began to appear. In many cases, as with this example, the image on the card is in fact the *Olympic*. Her bow name has been erased and that of the *Titanic* clumsily substituted on the photographic negative.

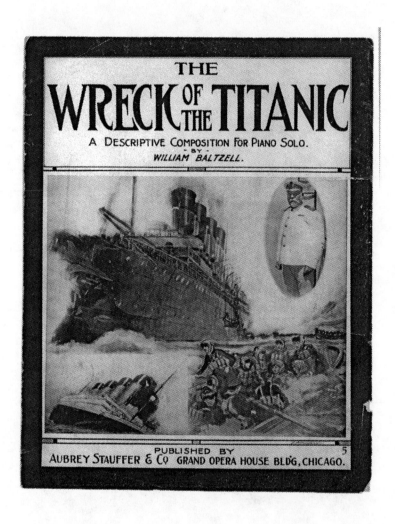

Postcards were not the only items produced to attempt to cash in on the *Titanic* disaster. Also marketed were numerous poorly written pieces of sheet music. On the flipside of this particular piece, there is a dedication to the *Titanic's* "brave musicians."

Perhaps the most common of the post-disaster memorial products were books purporting to report the 'true' facts surrounding the sinking of the *Titanic*. Printed with a variety of cover colors, these books were anything but accurate, containing many specious theories and outright falsehoods. Today, many people owning these 1912 memorial editions believe them to be very rare and valuable. In actuality, they are not, as literally tens of thousands of the volumes were printed.

In both Britain and the United States, a number of commemorative plaques and monuments were erected to honour the heroes of the *Titanic* disaster. This memorial, for the *Titanic's* senior wireless operator Jack Phillips, was constructed in part with funds raised by the Postal Telegraph Clerks Association.

Ongoing efforts to provide aid to families touched by the disaster resulted in numerous benefit concerts and fund-raising events. The pictured programme is from one such benefit function, presented by the Royal Opera of Covent Garden.

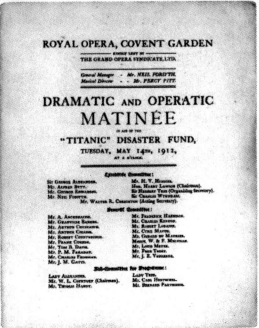

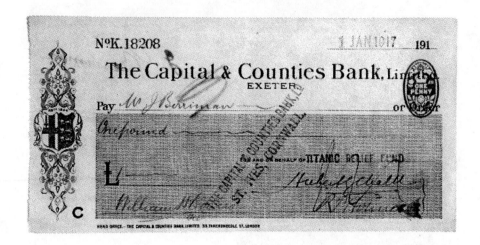

To effectively distribute money to individuals affected by the *Titanic* disaster, several assistance funds were set up. One of the most enduring of these was officially called the Titanic Relief Fund and was located in the UK. This cheque was drawn on that same fund and was made payable to the brother of a *Titanic* victim.

Tributes to those lost on the *Titanic* sometimes took on a very personal tone. This cigarette case was presented to survivor Henry Harper by the widow of *Titanic* victim Howard Case. Engraved into the front of the silver-plated case were the initials "H.H.," and the date when the gift was presented, August 1912. Also pictured, accompanying the case, is a note written by Mrs. Harper which explains the sentiments behind the presentation of the gift.

For the men who actually built the *Titanic*, the loss of the ship was a very emotional blow. Out of desire to remember the vessel into which they had poured so much of their labour, many of the men who worked at the Harland and Wolff shipyard in Belfast took home articles associated with the construction job. The square of red fabric pictured above came from the end of a roll which was used to upholster the chairs for one of the *Titanic's* dining lounges. The textile scrap was taken home and preserved by one of the paymasters who worked at Harland and Wolff.

About the Author

Steve Santini's fascination with the *Titanic* began when, as a young boy, he viewed the classic British film, *A Night to Remember*. This experience spawned an interest in the ship which has led Santini into over two decades of research into the doomed ocean liner and the events surrounding her sinking.

Today, many consider Santini one of Canada's leading *Titanic* researchers. He has lectured at numerous museums, appeared on national media forums, and consulted on various film and documentary projects including James Cameron's blockbuster film, *Titanic*. In 1999, Santini co-authored *The Science and Story of Titanic*, published by Somerville House, a division of Penguin/Putnam.

Presently, Santini holds the positions of historian and research associate at the Manitoba Museum of the Titanic—Canada's largest assemblage of *Titanic*-related artifacts. Also a consulting historian for the Canadian Titanic Society, Santini is often called upon to examine and authenticate *Titanic* memorabilia and relics for museums and private collections worldwide.

*

Craig A. Sopin owns one of the largest privately held *Titanic* collections in North America. Pieces from his collection have often been lent out to museums and have been featured in all forms of media, including the 1998 Simon and Schuster book, *Titanic: Fortune and*

Fate. Lecturing frequently on the topic, Sopin's expertise is in the field of *Titanic* collectibles is regularly sought out by auction houses, museums, dealers, and collectors. When his *Titanic* activities permit, Sopin practices law in Pennsylvania.

Research and Artifact Sources

All of the artifact images and historical information contained in the this book were acquired from the archives and artifact collections of Titanic Concepts Inc. and the Manitoba Museum of the Titanic. To view more of the Titanic Concepts Inc. collection, visit the Manitoba Museum of the Titanic on-line at: *www.titanicconcepts.com*

All images, photographic and otherwise, appearing in this publication are the sole property of Titanic Concepts Inc. and the Manitoba Museum of the Titanic and are copyright protected. The images may not be reproduced in any manner without prior written permission from Titanic Concepts Inc.. Any party or parties using information, photos, and/or excerpts from this publication without written permission will be in violation of copyright law and will be prosecuted to the fullest extent allowable by law.

Index

CPSIA information can be obtained at www.ICGtesting.com
Printed in the USA
LVOW071941220911

247433LV00001B/325/A